WHAT IS THE SCIENTIFIC METHOD?

SCIENCE BOOK FOR KIDS
CHILDREN'S SCIENCE BOOKS

BABY PROFESSOR
EDUCATION KIDS

Speedy Publishing LLC

40 E. Main St. #1156

Newark, DE 19711

www.speedypublishing.com

Copyright 2017

In this book, we're going to talk about the scientific method. So, let's get right to it!

WHAT IS THE SCIENTIFIC METHOD?

The Scientific Method is a system that scientists use to create and try experiments. The process is designed to minimize errors in experiments. If you follow the steps properly, it helps you feel confident that your results are accurate, and if you performed the experiment again, you would be able to repeat your results.

FEMALE SCIENTIST WORKING IN LABORATORY

All experiments start with an observation and a question you want to answer.

Suppose you planted two flowering plants in your backyard. You give the plants the same amount of water and it seems like they are getting the same amount of sun. However, the first plant is doing really well and the second one isn't thriving and you don't know why. You might decide to conduct a soil experiment to see if the soil in the area of your backyard where the first plant was planted is different than the area where the second plant is planted.

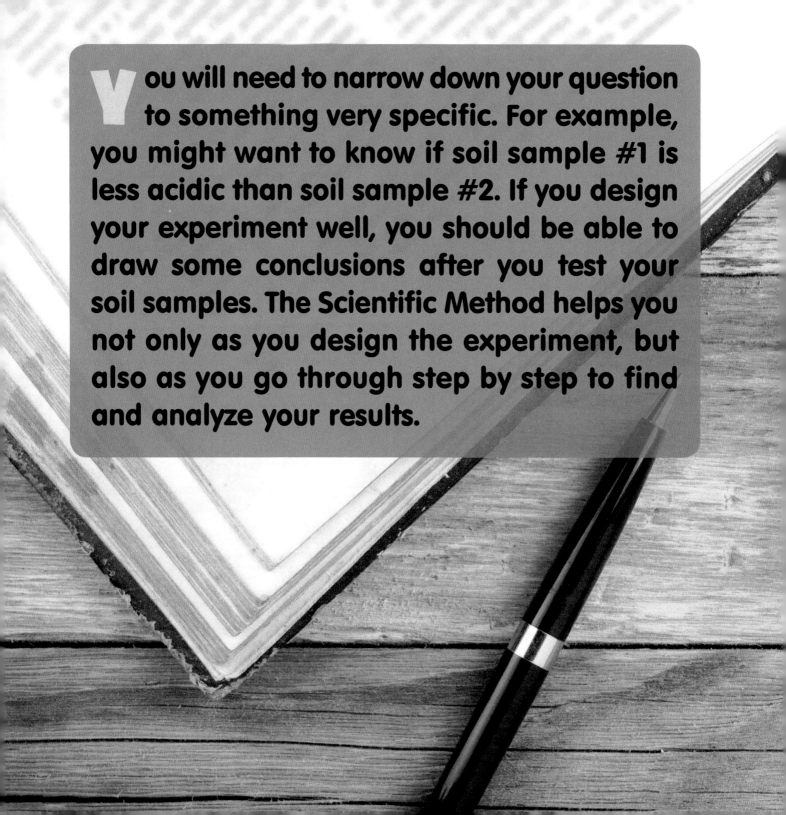

You will need to narrow down your question to something very specific. For example, you might want to know if soil sample #1 is less acidic than soil sample #2. If you design your experiment well, you should be able to draw some conclusions after you test your soil samples. The Scientific Method helps you not only as you design the experiment, but also as you go through step by step to find and analyze your results.

The Scientific Method uses a step-by-step logical process. It eliminates the need for just guessing and gives you a method to obtain facts and data to prove or disprove your theory or hypothesis.

THE THEORY OF RELATIVITY, ALBERT EINSTEIN

THE HISTORY OF THE SCIENTIFIC METHOD

The method we know today as the Scientific Method wasn't invented by just one scientist. The process was proposed by different scientists. It was discussed and debated for many centuries until it became a standard that all scientists use.

SIR FRANCIS BACON

Many scientists contributed to the thought process behind the Scientific Method but there were three in particular who contributed a great deal to it. They were:

- Francis Bacon (1561-1626), who was an English philosopher

- Rene Descartes (1596-1650), who was a French mathematician and scientist

- Isaac Newton (1643-1727), who was an English astronomer and physicist

Scientists continue to refine the ways in which they create and conduct experiments, but the structure and process they follow has been standardized and is followed by scientists around the world.

ISAAC NEWTON

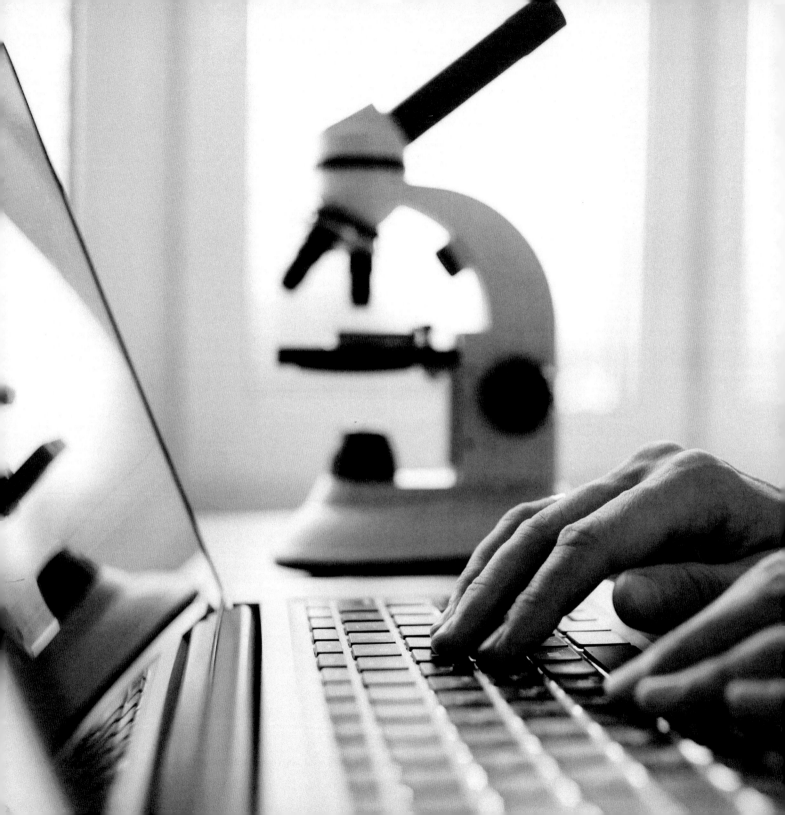

STEPS IN THE SCIENTIFIC METHOD

The Scientific Method is based on a logical procedure of steps so that you can come to a conclusion once you've performed your experiment. It helps you to organize your thinking and your resulting data.

STEP 1: Observe to determine what you want to uncover or find out.

STEP 2: Develop a theory or hypothesis about what you believe is true.

STEP 3: Predict what your results might be. If my theory or hypothesis is true, then I predict this will be the correct conclusion.

YOUNG BOY OBSERVES THROUGH MAGNIFYING GLASS

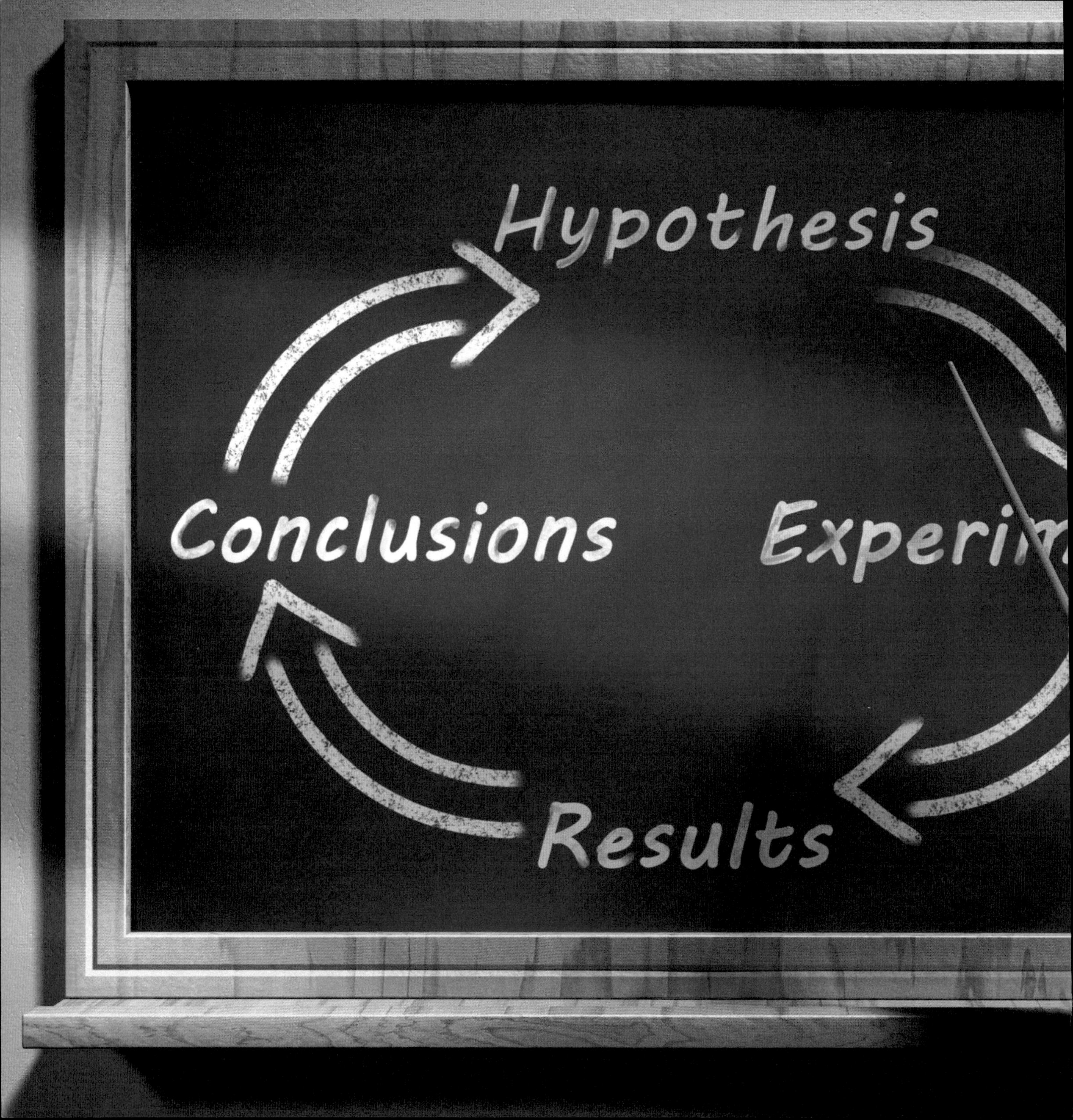
Hypothesis
Conclusions
Results

STEP 4: Conduct the experiment that you have designed to test your hypothesis.

STEP 5: Organize and analyze your findings and summarize a conclusion.

This may seem complicated, but after you've conducted one or two experiments using these guidelines, it will become second nature.

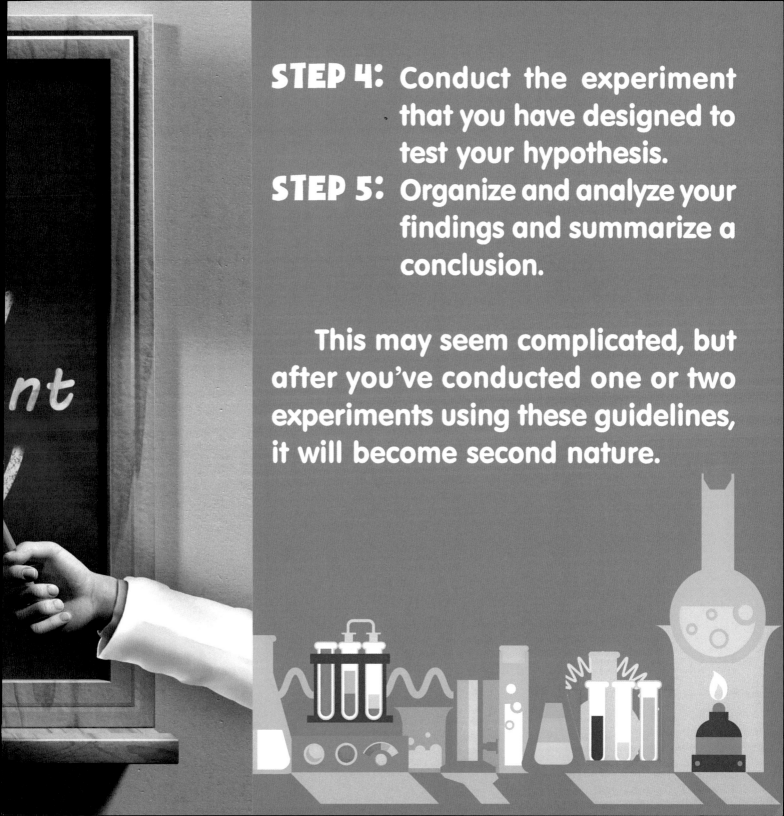

OBSERVATION

This step usually involves research. After you have chosen a specific topic for your experiment and a detailed question that you want to answer, you'll need to research as much material as possible about it. For example, for the plant experiment, you'll want to know all the factors that could possibly impact the growth of your plants.

BOY CHECKING YOUNG SEEDLING PLANT

GREEN PLANTS AND SCIENTIFIC EQUIPMENT IN BIOLOGY LABOROTARY

You might want to know more about the biology of the plants and the factors that lead to plant growth. You might want to consider whether something is happening to one plant and not the other that isn't obvious from direct observation. You think it might be a difference in the soil, but is there anything else that could be causing the problem?

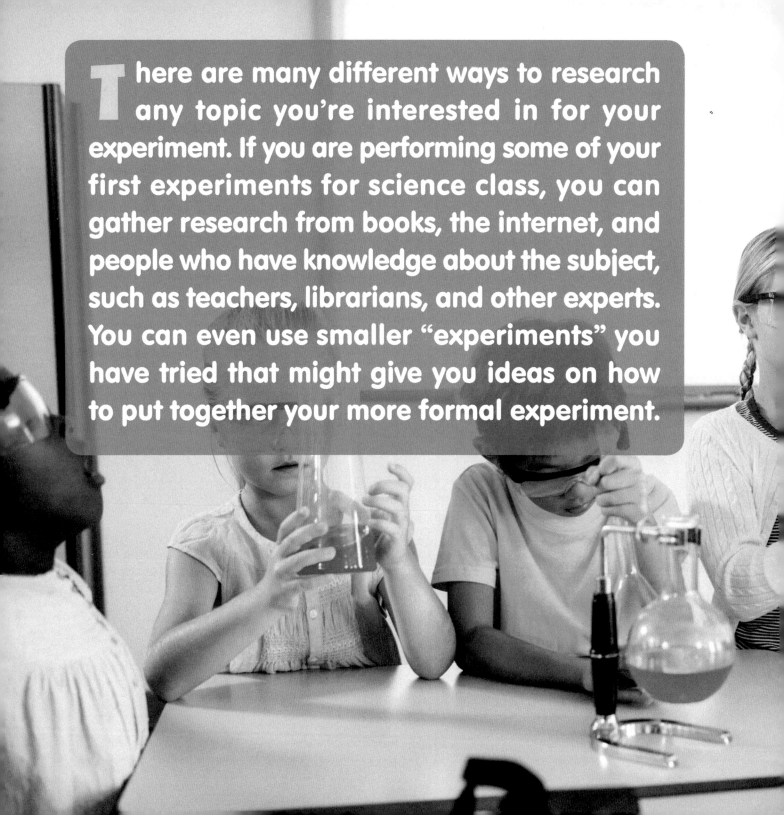

There are many different ways to research any topic you're interested in for your experiment. If you are performing some of your first experiments for science class, you can gather research from books, the internet, and people who have knowledge about the subject, such as teachers, librarians, and other experts. You can even use smaller "experiments" you have tried that might give you ideas on how to put together your more formal experiment.

PUPILS DOING SCIENCE EXPERIMENT WITH A TEACHER IN CLASSROOM

BRAINSTORMING SESSION

HYPOTHESIS

Now that you have completed the research and "brainstorming" portion of your thinking, it's time to propose a theory or hypothesis for your experiment. You want this hypothesis to be simple and clear. Let's use the plants in your backyard as an example.

OBSERVATION: All other factors being equal, does the soil acidity affect the growth of plants?

HYPOTHESIS: "I think that the soil sample from plant 1 will be less acidic than the soil sample from plant 2 since plant 1 seems to be growing better than plant 2."

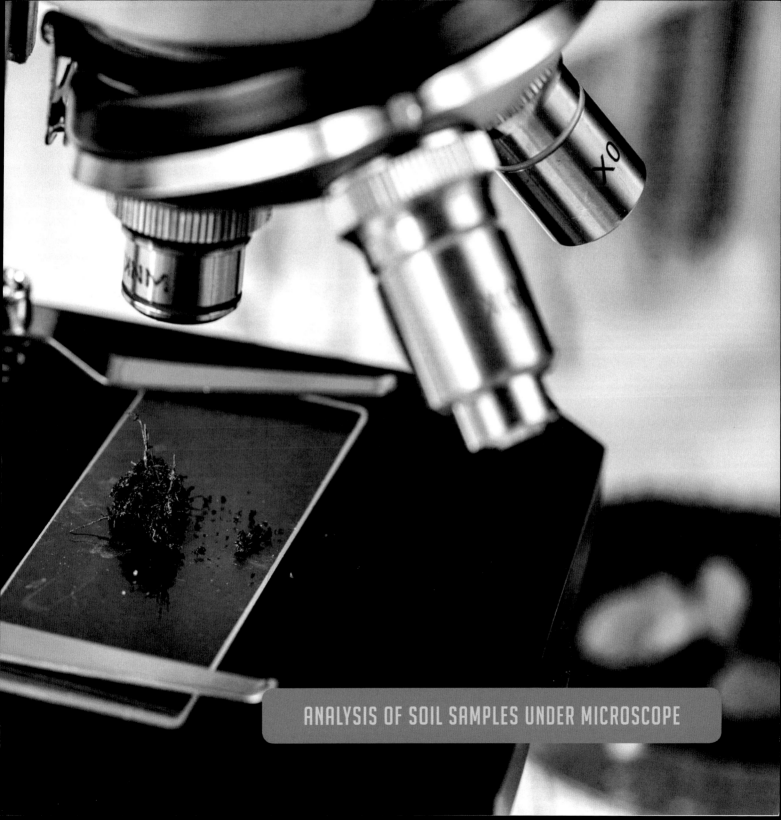

ANALYSIS OF SOIL SAMPLES UNDER MICROSCOPE

This hypothesis is based on the fact that most plants don't grow as well in highly acidic soil than less acidic soil. It's also based on the fact that the sunlight and water the plants are receiving appear to be the same and the plants don't seem to have any diseases or insect pests.

Your well-thought-out hypothesis should give you a concise idea of what you think is happening during the process of your observations.

PREDICTION

At this stage of the process, you will want to create a prediction that you can test. For example, with the experiment we've discussed, one possible prediction could be:

If I test the soil under plant 2, I expect it to be 20% more acidic than the soil under plant 1.

WOMAN BIOLOGIST HOLDING TEST TUBE

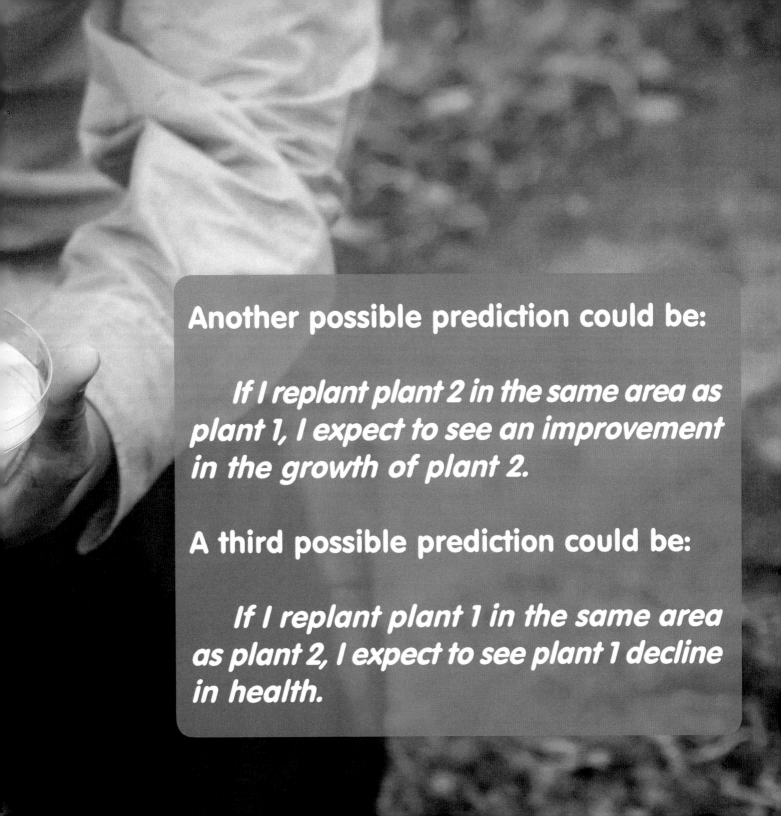

Another possible prediction could be:

    If I replant plant 2 in the same area as plant 1, I expect to see an improvement in the growth of plant 2.

A third possible prediction could be:

    If I replant plant 1 in the same area as plant 2, I expect to see plant 1 decline in health.

The prediction you decide upon will help you to decide how you are going to conduct the experiment. It's very important to remember that if your prediction doesn't turn out to be true, it doesn't mean that your experiment has failed. It just means that your experiment may have brought some other facts to light that also have to be tested.

SCARED YOUNG SCIENTIST LOOKING AT THE OVERFLOWING FOAM

In fact, some of the greatest scientific discoveries of all time have happened when specific theories and predictions have been proven by experimentation that they were NOT correct. When this happens, scientists must dig deeper and approach their experiment or experiments in a different way to discover new truths and form new hypotheses.

A prediction that turns out false doesn't mean that you have failed as a scientist!

EXPERIMENT

Now it's time for the actual experiment to start. You decide to go with your first prediction. You are going to run a test on the two soil samples to see if the sample under plant 2 is 20% more acidic than the soil under plant 1.

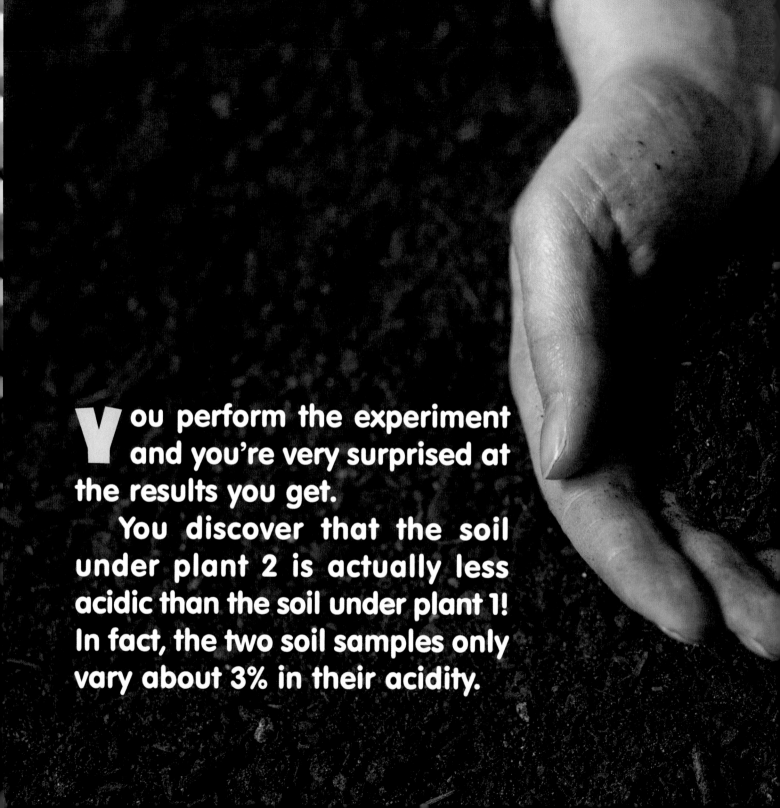

You perform the experiment and you're very surprised at the results you get.

You discover that the soil under plant 2 is actually less acidic than the soil under plant 1! In fact, the two soil samples only vary about 3% in their acidity.

Your original prediction is incorrect. Remember, you haven't failed. It just means that the variable you thought was causing the problem, a possible variance in the soil, may or may not be causing the problem. Perhaps this type of plant thrives in a soil that's more acidic. It's possible that if you make the soil more acidic, the plants will do even better! You'll have to go back to the drawing board and think about what other variables might be causing plant 2 to not be growing as well as plant 1.

It's important to remember that it's rarely possible to prove a theory by conducting just one experiment. The idea is to test and refine, test and refine, and test and refine again, until you have enough data and feel absolutely certain that another scientist would get the same results that you did if he or she conducted the same experiment.

SUCCESSFUL INVENTOR AT HIS DESK WITH EQUIPMENT

Master scientists keep careful records of their data so that others can study their results and try to prove or disprove their theories.

SHELVES FULL OF FILES

CONCLUSION

The last step for this particular experiment is to form your conclusion. This will be the summary of the data you collected and the final result for this first experiment.

You only have two different options.

OPTION 1: The original hypothesis was supported by the findings of this experiment.

OPTION 2: The original hypothesis was NOT supported by the findings of this experiment.

The important thing to remember is that even if your results had supported your original hypothesis, it doesn't mean you would have proved your hypothesis to be true. Experiments can always have flaws so you have to repeat an experiment more than once to prove your findings and other scientists would have to be able to get the same results you did too.

An experiment is only a failure if it doesn't control the variables you want to test or doesn't provide data that helps you to answer your original question.

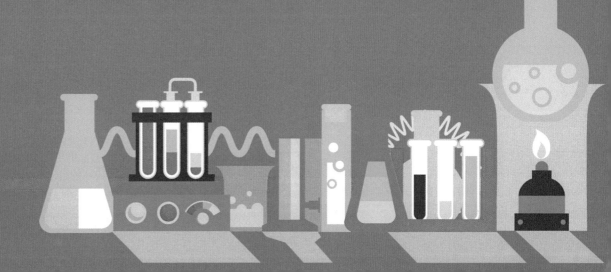

Awesome! Now you know more about the scientific method. You can find more Science books from Baby Professor by searching the website of your favorite book retailer.

Visit

BABY PROFESSOR
EDUCATION KIDS

www.BabyProfessorBooks.com

to download Free Baby Professor eBooks
and view our catalog of new and exciting
Children's Books

Made in the USA
Las Vegas, NV
24 April 2021

21901051R00040